FROM THE MEDES TO THE MULLAHS

A History of Iran

by Anne Davison

Copyright 2013 Anne Davison

Books for Busy People

Other Books in the 'In Brief' Series by Anne Davison

Abraham's Children: Jew Christian Muslim, Commonality and Conflict

Holy Roman Empire: Power Politics Papacy

Making Sense of Militant Islam

Paul of Tarsus: a First Century Radical

The Ottoman Empire

All available at Amazon

****

TABLE OF CONTENTS

PREFACE	5
INTRODUCTION	6
CHAPTER 1 ANCIENT EMPIRES	8
The Medes and Achaemenids	8
The Graeco/Persian Wars	10
Philip II and Alexander of Macedonia	12
Zoroastrianism	14
CHAPTER 2 FROM HELLENISM TO ISLAM	17
The Seleucids and Parthians	17
The Roman/Parthian Wars	18
The Sassanids	20
The Islamic Conquest	23
The Sunni/Shi'a Schism	24

CHAPTER 3 MUSLIM MONARCHIES — 26

    The Abbasids — 26

    The Mongols — 29

    The Safavids — 30

    The Qajars — 33

CHAPTER 4 THE MODERN PERIOD — 35

    World War I — 35

    The Pahlavi Dynasty — 35

    The Iranian Revolution — 38

    The Iran-Iraq War — 40

    A Nuclear Threat? — 42

EPILOGUE — 44

ABOUT THE AUTHOR — 47

Preface

The content of this short book began as a series of lectures. At the time, I was often asked if I had ever written on the subject and over a period of time I was encouraged by others to bring the material together as a book.

What follows is an overview of the history of Iran, starting around 670 BCE with the period of the Medes and ending with the modern Islamic Republic of Iran. The book is aimed at the general reader rather than the academic. I start with the big picture, the outline, and then fill in some, but not all, of the detail. It is rather like building a house; beginning with the frame, then dividing the interior into different rooms and finally putting the furniture in place.

Occasionally I will include events that are not perhaps central to Iranian history, for example the Battle of Marathon or the meeting of Anthony and Cleopatra in Tarsus, modern Turkey. The reason for their inclusion is because I have tried to make links between events that are familiar to readers of European history with the history of Iran. In other words, fitting the pieces of 'Western' history into the larger jigsaw of world history. My hope is that the reader may be encouraged to furnish the rooms, or discover some other pieces of the jigsaw for themselves.

A word about dating: I have used BCE (Before the Common/Current Era) rather than BC and I have retained the more familiar AD. However, from Chapter Three onwards I have dropped the use of AD since by this time the period should be obvious to the reader and repeated, unnecessary, use could be irritating.

The book was first published in 2013. This version provides an extended Epilogue in order to bring the situation in Iran in relation to the current Syrian crisis and changes in world politics, up to date.

Introduction

Throughout much of its history the country of Iran has also been referred to as Persia. Both names have been used at various times to describe this region of central Asia and both names will be used throughout according to context. The name Iran takes its roots from the word Aryan and from about 600 BCE the region was known as the 'Land of the Aryans'. The word Persia was used by the Greeks to describe the tribal people who lived in the area of Pars, or Fars in South Western Iran. In common with the Greeks, the Biblical writers also spoke of Persia. The language Farsi, or Parsee, is also derived from the region of Pars, as are the Parsees of India. Since the 1979 AD Revolution the country has been officially known as the Islamic Republic of Iran and most people of the country refer to themselves as Iranians.

In order to understand the history of any country it is helpful to look first at its geography. Geography determines trade and relations with neighbouring countries and geography also influences the movement of people and ideas. Topography is also important because mountains and rivers provide both a natural defense and a deterrent to invaders. If we look at the map of Iran we can see the natural boundaries of the Persian Gulf, the Zagros mountains and the mountainous regions of Afghanistan. At various times in history the boundary of what was Greater Iran reached the Caspian Sea in the North West, the Levant in the West and the Indus Valley in the East.

In the early part of its history the ancient Silk Road stretched across the northern part of Greater Iran, carrying both goods and ideas between Egypt and China, bringing both wealth and power to the region. As early as 500 BCE a postal system operated along the route providing fresh horses and riders at regular intervals.

Iran's political history has also been entwined with that of its neighbours and events in the wider region. In the East, relations with the Afghans, the Mongols and people of the Indian sub-continent have varied from one of friendly alliance to open hostility. In the West, relations with Imperial Rome, the Byzantines, the Islamic Caliphates, the Ottomans and Russia have often been volatile. In recent years Iran has experienced tensions not only with near neighbours Israel, Saudi Arabia and Iraq, but also with those further afield such as the United States and the United Kingdom.

Another point worth mentioning is that world maps change; names change and so do boundaries. If you look at a map of Iran today, you will not see many of those ancient names such as Susa, Haran or Babylon. Furthermore, Iran today is much smaller than it has been for most of its history when it incorporated todays Iraq, Afghanistan and regions bordering the Caspian Sea. Changing boundaries are usually the consequence of, or reason for, conflict and war. There have been border conflicts with Russia, Afghanistan, the Ottomans and Turkey and more recently with Iraq.

Two other points that are relevant to Iran's recent past. First, it has vast oil and gas reserves and second, it is a Shi'a country surrounded by an often-hostile Sunni Islam.

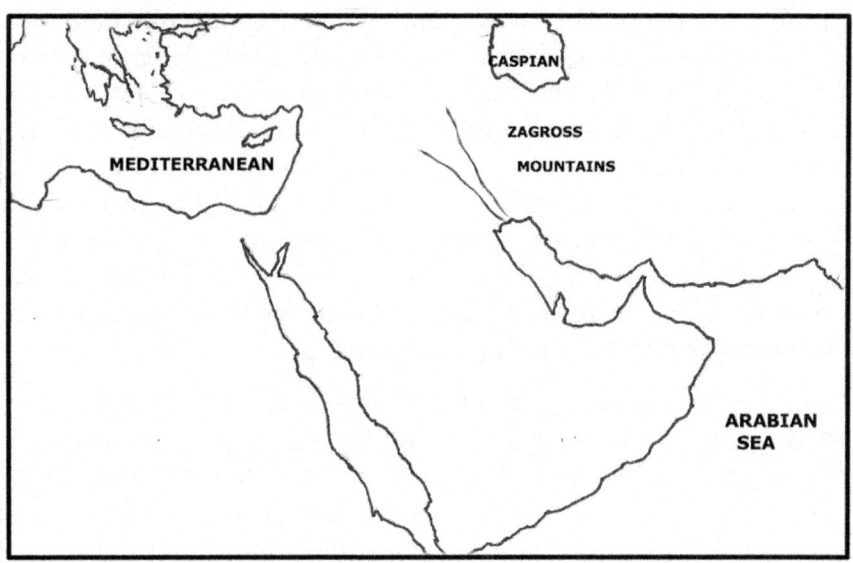

Chapter 1 Ancient Empires

The Medes and the Achaemenids

We begin with the Median Empire, or Median Confederation, which lasted from 678 BCE to 549 BCE. Before this time the Medes and also the Persians came under the rule of the Neo Assyrian Empire which was based in Mesopotamia, modern day Iraq. The Medes, the Assyrians and Mesopotamia are all mentioned in the Bible and it was sometime between 597 BCE and 582 BCE when, according to the Hebrew Scriptures, that Nebuchadnezzar, King of the Neo Babylonian Empire sacked Jerusalem and deported thousands of Jews to Babylon, which was located near to modern Baghdad. This event is sometimes referred to as the First Jewish Diaspora.

In 538 BCE Cyrus the Great, ruler of the Median Empire, which became known as the Achaemenid Empire, conquered Babylonia. He then freed the Jews, many of whom returned to Jerusalem where they began building the Second Temple. However, not all Jews returned; a considerable number remained in Babylonia and their descendants eventually became a sizeable Iraqi Jewish community, a remnant of which can still be found in Baghdad. The return of the Jews from their exile in Babylon is a pivotal moment in Jewish history and is remembered by Jews around the world in their prayers when they give thanks to Cyrus the Great for the freedom he gave them some two and a half thousand years ago.

Cyrus was from Pars and was the first ruler of the first great Persian, or Achaemenid Dynasty. His Empire was vast, stretching from modern day Turkey in the West to the Indus Valley in the East. He is remembered as a just ruler and part of his success was due to his tolerance towards those he conquered, allowing freedom of religion and also an element of self-rule. He replaced the client kings of the Median period with twenty *satraps* who ruled the Empire as viceroys, or governors in the name of the Emperor. The *satraps* were responsible for the administration of land and highways, collecting taxes and acting as judges. It was a system that was later inherited by successive Empires.

We have some evidence of Cyrus's rule from the famous Cyrus Cylinder that is now housed in the British Museum. Written in cuneiform, an ancient form of wedge shaped script that was first used by the Akkadians and Sumerians around 2000 BCE, the cylinder describes the good deeds of Cyrus. It tells how he had improved the lives of the citizens of Babylonia, repatriated displaced peoples such as the Jews and restored temples and cult sanctuaries. The inscriptions on the cylinder have been described by the United Nations as 'an ancient declaration of human rights'. Cyrus is considered by many Iranians today as the 'Father' of the nation of Iran, the founder of the great Achaemenid Empire of ancient times; far greater than Alexander the Great.

Many Iranians look back with pride to the pre-Islamic period. In 1971 AD the last Pahlavi Shah of Persia, Mohammad Reza Shah, organised a spectacular ceremony to commemorate the 2,500th year anniversary of the founding of the Achaemenid Empire. The event took over ten years to plan and the Cyrus Cylinder formed part of the logo. Fifty luxury tents were erected around a central fountain on the site of ancient Persepolis. It has been suggested that the *Field of the Cloth of Gold*, the meeting place of Francis I of France and Henry VIII of England in 1520 AD, inspired the Shah's tent city. The tents included a *Tent of Honour* for receiving dignitaries plus a vast *Banqueting Hall* and the whole area was surrounded by magnificent gardens. Maxims of Paris provided the catering. Not surprisingly the people criticized the Shah for his extravagance, which was just one example of the growing anti-Shah feeling that eventually led to his downfall.

Cyrus the Great died in battle in December 530 BCE. The remains of what is believed to be his tomb still exist in Pasargadae near Pars in Iran. Greek and Roman accounts give a detailed description of the tomb, which was surrounded by beautiful gardens. The coffin was made of gold and the interior of the tomb was completely decorated with fine carpets and tapestries. Apparently during the period of Alexander the Great's campaign the tomb was robbed of its finery by some of his soldiers. When Alexander later visited the tomb he was horrified and blamed the *Magi*, members of a priestly cult of the Mazdian religion, who were given responsibility for protecting the site. The tomb is now a World Heritage Site and visited by thousands of tourists each year.

Another great leader of the Achaemenid Empire was Darius the Great, who ruled from 522 BCE to 486 BCE. During this period the Empire was at its greatest extent, stretching from Egypt to the Balkans and across to today's Pakistan in the East. Darius continued the system of government by *satraps* that had been put in place by Cyrus. He decreed that Aramaic should be the common language but that the people of Persis, the Persians, should have their own Aryan language that was to be used specifically for official documents. He devised a new monetary system and built great palaces, towns and cities including Susa and Persepolis, meaning the City of the Persians. This was also a period of cultural achievement and some very fine art, particularly Achaemenid pieces of inlaid silver in bronze work, can be found in museums around the world today.

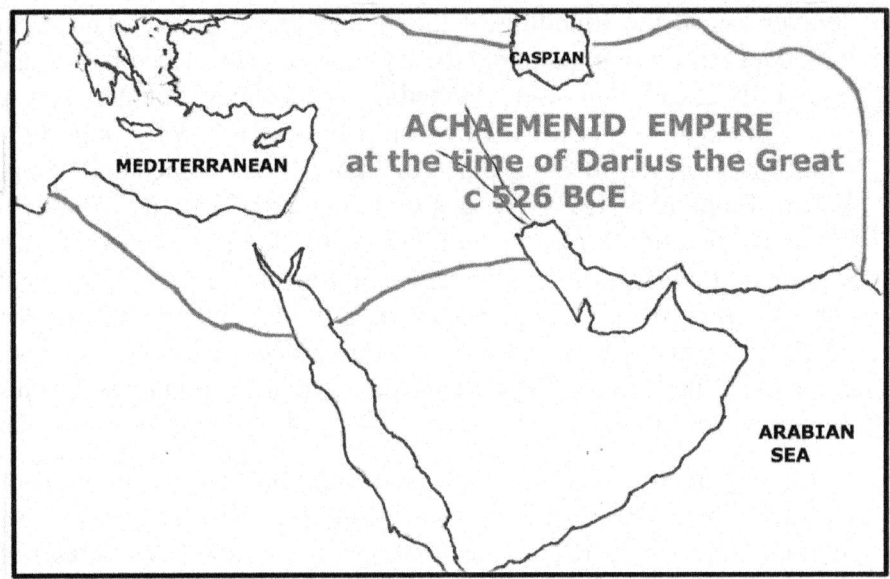

The Graeco-Persian Wars

During the reign of Darius I many of the people who lived on the islands and coastline on the Persian side of the Aegean Sea were Greeks living under Persian rule. With encouragement from mainland Greeks, the Persian Greeks rebelled against their Persian overlords in what is known as the Ionian Revolt that took place between 499 BCE and 493 BCE. The revolt was brutally put down by the Persians and in 492 BCE Darius went further by invading the Greek mainland.

The Persians were over optimistic. At the famous Battle of Marathon in 490 BCE Darius's vast army, which modern estimates place at between 25,000 and 100,000 Infantry, was firmly beaten by a much smaller, better-equipped and well-disciplined Athenian army of some 10,000 Infantry. According to legend a runner named Pheidippides, some accounts say Philippides, then ran the 25 miles from the battle scene to Athens with news of victory. After proclaiming victory before the King, he collapsed and died. Other accounts say that Pheidippides ran some 140 miles over two days to Sparta and back with a request for their help. Whatever the truth may be, the event is still with us. It gave rise to the modern marathon that was introduced at the 1896 AD Athens Olympic Games and takes place today in many parts of the world.

Darius the Great died in 486 BCE while planning a second invasion of Greece. He was buried in a rock tomb at *Naqsh-e Rustam*, an ancient necropolis located near Persepolis that became the burial place of several Achaemenid kings.

At the age of 36 Xerxes I, the son of Darius, succeeded his father. In 480 BCE Xerxes led a second invasion of Greece that included both land and sea forces gathered from across the Persian Empire. It has been suggested that as many as 2 million combatants from 47 ethnic groups made up the Persian forces including some 300 to 400 ships. Xerxes faced an allied force of Athenians and Spartans, which, though smaller in number, included the famed hoplite warriors who were better-armed and more skillful fighters than the Persians. Once more the Persians were defeated, this time during two sea battles; the Battle of Salamis and the Battle of Plataea. The Persians were soon on the defensive and by the end of 479 BCE, they were finally pushed out of Europe.

These battles marked a turning point in the Graeco/Persian wars. From now on Greece would become the rising power in the Eastern Mediterranean, and indeed beyond. In fact, many historians believe that the Battles of Salamis and Plataea were pivotal to European history. Had the Persians been victorious over the Greeks it is conceivable that Persian culture rather than Greek culture would have formed the basis of Western civilization.

Two other points worth mentioning at this stage: a) these ancient conflicts in the Aegean between the Greeks and the Persians have, intermittently, continued into modern times. For example, the Turks, who are heirs of the Persians in terms of territory, are still in conflict with Greece over the island of Cyprus, b) the battle between the Greeks and the Persians in the 5th Century BCE could also be seen as perhaps the first major confrontation between the Eastern and Western civilisations.

Philip II and Alexander of Macedonia

Despite the fact that the Greeks had defeated the Persians at the battles of Marathon, Salamis and Plataea, the Persian threat remained. The invasions of Darius and his son Xerxes had threatened both Greek civilization and Greek sovereignty. They vowed therefore not only to get their revenge, but to completely annihilate the Persian empire. However, at the time, in 497 BCE, they faced two problems; first the Greek city-states were fighting among themselves, a situation that led to the Peloponnesian Wars that raged between 431 BCE and 404 BCE and second, they lacked a capable leader who could both unite the warring factions and lead an effective invasion against Persia.

The person who finally came to take on this role was Philip II, the youngest son of King Amyntas of Macedon. As a young boy Philip had been held hostage in Thebes, which was then the leading city of Greece where he received a sound military and diplomatic training. He came to the Macedonian throne in 359 BCE when he was about 23 years old. Soon after his accession Philip embarked upon a campaign that united the previously disparate Greek city-states. Philip's next ambition was to invade and conquer Persia. However, in 336 BCE while preparing for the invasion, he was assassinated and was succeeded by his son Alexander II, known as Alexander the Great.

Alexander, who is often described as the greatest military leader of all time, was born in 356 BCE. As a young boy, he was placed under the tutelage of the famous philosopher Aristotle. Once he became king he took on his father's mission to conquer the Persians. The fact that Philip II had already laid down plans for the invasion and had amassed powerful armies worked to the advantage of Alexander.

Early in 334 BCE Alexander crossed the Hellespont, the narrow stretch of water that separates Europe from Asia in modern Istanbul with approximately 48,000 soldiers, 6,000 Cavalry and a fleet of 120 ships. The first major engagement took place in May 334 BCE at the Battle of Granicus a short distance from the Hellespont. There were heavy casualties on both sides and Alexander himself was injured. However, the Greeks were victorious and they then moved further down the coast of Anatolia. The second, and decisive major battle took place in November 333 BCE at Issus in Southern Anatolia. Unlike at Granicus, when General Memnon of Rhodes led the Persian armies, this time the Persian King Darius III assumed command. However, once more Alexander was victorious and Darius and his armies fled in defeat. The ferocity of the battle and fear on the face of Darius is well portrayed in a famous mosaic that is today housed in the Naples National Archaeological Museum.

Now there was no stopping Alexander. From Issus he continued down the coast of modern Syria and Lebanon and into Egypt where he founded the city of Alexandria. He then retraced his steps back towards Persia and crossed Asia Minor as far as modern day Afghanistan and Pakistan. If a city surrendered, the buildings and its inhabitants were spared in exchange for the payment of taxes and acceptance of vassal status. If a city refused to surrender it was razed to the ground and the inhabitants either massacred or taken into slavery. One such city to suffer this fate was the ancient city of Persepolis that had been built by Darius I and was the pride of the Persian people. It is thought that in the midst of a drinking bout Alexander ordered the burning of the city in revenge for the Persian burning of Athens.

The excavated site of ancient Persepolis is today a popular tourist attraction and it is still possible to see some of the original reliefs depicting Persian, Median and Armenian soldiers that represent the multi-national nature of the Achaemenid Empire of Darius I.

In order to consolidate his Greek Empire Alexander encouraged his soldiers to marry local women and to settle and have children in the conquered countries. It is often said that today's blond, blue-eyed Persians and Afghans are a direct consequence of Alexander's campaigns. But he pushed himself and his armies far too hard and at the early age of 32, in the year 323 BCE, Alexander died in the palace of Nebuchadnezzar II in Babylon near today's Baghdad. Some say that he was poisoned, others that he died from his violent drinking; we will probably never know.

Alexander's body was taken to Memphis in Egypt by one of his generals, Ptolemy I. Ptolemy II then moved it to Alexandria where it remained until the reign of the Roman Emperor Caracalla in around 120 AD. Between Alexander's death and 120 AD, a period of some three hundred years, his tomb was visited by most of the Roman Emperors, all of whom admired Alexander greatly seeing him as the perfect military commander. Today there is no evidence of the original tomb but there is an excellent Alexander Sarcophagus, depicting the Battle of Issus, on display at the Istanbul Archaeology Museum.

The legacy of Alexander is not so much that he established a vast empire, but that his conquests resulted in the spread of Greek ideas, Greek philosophy, Greek religion and Greek culture, in other words Hellenism, from the Mediterranean to the Hindu Kush. Greek influence can also be seen in many Buddhists statues that have survived from this period. For example, in the Gandhara art that was produced in the region of modern Afghanistan, an area where archaeologists have also discovered remains of Greek style cities. Sadly, the Taliban recently destroyed some of the Buddhist statues. However, it is probably the use of the Greek language and culture that permeated across the empire that was to have the greatest effect on world history, as we shall see in a later chapter.

Zoroastrianism

The people of the ancient Iranian empires followed Mazdaism or Magianism, which was an early form of Zoroastrianism. Zoroastrianism remained the predominant Faith until the arrival of Islam in the 6th Century AD. After the Islamic Conquest many

Zoroastrians fled to India where they are known as Parsis, taking their name from Pars in ancient Persia.

Zoroastrianism is based on the teaching of the prophet Zoroaster, also known as Zarathustra, which was his name in his native language of *Avestan*. He is said to have lived in North Eastern Iran sometime between 1500 BCE and 600 BCE. Zoroastrianism is therefore one of the oldest religions in the world and it is thought that some of its ideas influenced Judaism, Christianity and Islam. What little evidence we have of early Zoroastrianism is drawn from the *Avesta*, sacred texts which were compiled over several centuries starting perhaps as early as 500 BCE. Many of these early texts, which comprised hymns and prayers, were lost at the time of Alexander the Great's campaign and the destruction of Persepolis in the 4th Century BCE, but some survived and were later compiled into a formal canon under the Sassanids in the 4th Century AD. Another source for our knowledge of early Zoroastrianism is from the *Histories of Herodotus*.

Zoroaster was born into a priestly family at a time when the Aryan religion, or Brahmanism, was prevalent in the region from Iran to the Indus Valley. According to tradition, when Zoroaster was about 30, he went into the river to draw water and when he emerged he claimed to have received a revelation from *Ahura Mazda*, the one supreme God of Zoroastrians. This experience is similar to that of Guru Nanak, founder of the Sikh religion in the 15th Century AD, who also emerged from a river announcing that he had received a revelation from God.

The event was life-changing for Zoroaster and from this moment on he travelled around preaching and teaching the message of *Ahura Mazda*; the fundamental message being that people should stop worshipping many gods and devote their lives to the one true God, *Ahura Mazda* the sole creator of the universe, the source of all goodness who is worthy of the highest worship. According to Zoroastrians *Ahura Mazda* has two attributes; *Ahura* meaning Being and *Mazda* meaning Mind. He is Ultimate Being, Uncreated, all Pure and all True. He is the creator of all that is good, while all that is evil emanates from *Angra Mainyu*, the destructive spirit. Fundamental to Zoroastrianism is that all creation is in conflict between the good

Spirit, *Ahura Mazda* and the evil Spirit, *Angra Mainya*. Humans should therefore strive to base their lives on good deeds in order to ensure a happy life and keep evil at bay. Ritual purity plays a key role in Zoroastrian worship and fire and water are major elements that are both purifying, life-sustaining and symbolizing spiritual wisdom.

Zoroastrians also believe that after death there will be a Day of Judgment and consignment to either Heaven or Hell. Furthermore, at the end times a savior figure, the *Soashyant*, will appear who will redeem the world and raise the dead. It can be seen that there are clear analogies with later monotheistic religions.

A practice that is unique to Zoroastrians is the process for dealing with the dead. Because it is believed that a dead body is corrupt it is never buried because a dead body would pollute the earth, which is sacred. Even the ashes of a cremated body can pollute the soil. The traditional practice therefore is to place the body in the open air, usually on top of a tower known as the Tower of Silence, where it is exposed to the elements and particularly the vultures. In time the body is stripped of its flesh by the birds of prey and the bones are scorched by the sun and wind. Only then are the bones put into a small ossuary pit the bottom of the burial mound.

Today there are possibly no more than 200,000 Zoroastrians worldwide, the majority of whom live in Mumbai, India where they still place their dead on the Tower of Silence. Zoroastrianism as the established religion of Persia was virtually wiped out in the 7th Century with the arrival of Islam. However, many elements have survived and are incorporated into the culture of today's Iran. For example, four of the main festivals celebrated by Iranians today focus on the victory of light over darkness. The most important festival is the Iranian New Year, known as Nowruz, which marks the arrival of light, new birth and the revival of nature. Other elements of Zoroastrianism, such as the importance of speaking the truth and a deep sense of justice, have permeated down to the present time.

Chapter 2 From Hellenism to Islam

The Seleucids and Parthians

When Alexander the Great died unexpectedly at the early age of 32 his wife Roxana was pregnant with his son. When the child, known as Alexander IV Aegus, was born, his mother took him to Macedonia where mother and child lived under the protection of her mother-in-law Olympias. Despite such protection Roxana and her son were assassinated on the orders of Cassandra, a rival king claiming succession to the Greek Empire. With the death of the legitimate heir there followed a period of conflict between Alexander's various generals and other claimants to the throne.

As often happens in this situation, the Empire was divided up, the largest area coming under Seleucus I who founded the Seleucid Empire. Another important successor state was that of the Ptolemies, founded in Egypt by another of Alexander's generals, the Macedonian born Ptolemy I Soter. In 305 BCE Ptolemy I took the title of Pharaoh, so founding the Ptolemaic dynasty, which lasted until 30 BCE when the last Ptolemaic Pharaoh, Cleopatra the VII was defeated by the Romans.

The Seleucid Empire survived for almost three hundred years but it was too vast to maintain control and gradually fragmented, particularly around its borders. In the East, it lost territory to the Hindu Maurya dynasty of India and in the West the Empire was in constant conflict with the Ptolemies of Egypt, King Mithradates of Pontus and Armenia. It eventually faced the growing power of Rome.

However, the greatest threat was eventually to come from the Parni tribe of North Eastern Iran, which broke away from the Seleucids as early as 247 BCE and then went on to conquer Media and Mesopotamia. By 100 BCE the once great Seleucid Empire comprised little more than Antioch and surrounding region.

Being located on the ancient Silk Road, which stretched from the Mediterranean to China, the Parthian Empire became an important centre for trade and commerce and consequently grew in wealth. Culturally it incorporated both ancient Persian and Hellenistic influences and it established its capital at Ctesiphon, which is just South of today's Baghdad. While wanting to acknowledge its Greek Hellenistic culture, the Parthians were also proud of their ancient Persian, especially Achaemenid heritage. The first Parthian ruler, Arsaces I, saw himself in direct succession to Cyrus the Great and styled himself 'King of Kings, *Shahanshah*. It was a period of religious tolerance when people were free to worship the many Greek Gods of Hellenism, alongside Buddhism in the East, Judaism and later Christianity in the West, and of course Zoroastrianism.

The Parthians, as so many tribes from Central Asia, were great horsemen. It is sometimes said that they were more comfortable in the saddle than with their feet on the ground and that they were so connected to the horse that it was sometimes difficult to distinguish rider from animal. They were renowned for being able to fire scores of arrows backwards, in quick succession, while riding at great speed and it is from the Parthians that we get 'Parthian Shot', which evolved into the term 'parting shot'. Apart from light cavalry who used bows and arrows, the Parthians also had heavy cavalry with both rider and horse wearing heavy armour rather like Western Medieval knights.

The Roman/Parthian Wars

When the Parthians came to power in 247 BCE Rome was a relatively insignificant republic comprising little more than the Italian peninsula. By 30 BCE it had become an empire stretching across Europe and around the Mediterranean Sea to North Africa. On its Eastern border was Parthia, which presented both a threat and a challenge. The Roman Province of Syria acted as a buffer between the two competing powers.

The first serious encounter between the Parthians and the Romans came in 53 BCE at the Battle of Carrhae, another name for Haran. It is from Haran where, according to the Bible, Abraham with his relatives and livestock began their long journey towards Canaan some 4,000 years ago (Gen 12:5 NIV).

The Battle of Carrhae was significant because against all odds the smaller Parthian army defeated the invading Romans whose armies were led by the famous Marcus Licinius Crassus. Crassus was an extremely wealthy Roman politician who had earlier put down the slave revolt led by Spartacus in southern Italy. He was by this time governor of Syria and his ambition was to achieve military success in the East equal to that of Caesar in the West.

But despite having an army of 40,000, this was no match against the swiftness of the Parthian light cavalry and heavily armoured knights. The Romans were defeated; to the further dishonor of Rome the Parthians seized the battle standards and Legionary Eagles, which then became museum pieces in the capital city of Ctesiphon. Later, in 19 BCE, Emperor Augustus retrieved the standards as part of a peace treaty with the Parthians. However, in what might be described today as 'spin', when the standards were returned triumphantly to Rome the event was described as a victory over the Parthians rather than part of a peace treaty.

Following the defeat at Carrhae, Gaius Cassius Longinus led some 10,000 surviving soldiers back to Syria. Roman prisoners became slaves of the Parthians. Being renowned for their architectural and building skills they were put to work on the various Persian building projects, particularly bridges, roads and aqueducts at which they were expert. Many of the monuments in Iraq that survive from that period clearly show the Roman influence particularly when it comes to the Roman arch and forms of water supply.

It is believed that Crassus died in battle but there are various accounts of what had happened to him including being taken as a slave. The death of Crassus resulted in the end of the First Triumvirate, which was an informal political alliance between himself, Julius Caesar and Pompey the Great. The event also signaled the beginning of the civil wars between Caesar and Pompey. However, another man of equal, if not greater ambition, succeeded Crassus as Governor of the Eastern provinces. He was Marcus Antonius, better known to us as Mark Anthony, whose name will be forever linked with Cleopatra, the last of the Ptolemaic Pharaohs. As governor of the Eastern part of the Roman Republic he first met Cleopatra when he summoned her to meet him at Tarsus, on the coast of Anatolia in modern Turkey. The romanticized story of Anthony and Cleopatra is well known and was most famously portrayed in 1963 by Richard Burton and Elizabeth Taylor in the film 'Cleopatra'. Anthony continued the wars with the Parthians and he and Cleopatra also became involved in the Roman Civil Wars. But he was defeated by Augustus at the Battle of Actium in 31 BCE, at which point he and Cleopatra fled to Alexandria in Egypt where they committed suicide.

When Hadrian, the first Roman Emperor to sport a beard, succeeded Trajan in 117 AD he changed the earlier Roman policy of expansionism and instead worked for consolidation. Hadrian's policy was to secure the Empire's boundaries. At this point the Eastern boundary of the Roman Empire was Hatra, a small town located between Baghdad and Mosul in modern Iraq. Along its central European boundary, he extended and improved the fortifications along the rivers Rhine and Danube and he built the famous Hadrian's Wall in Northumberland, which marked the Northern-most boundary of the Roman Empire in the British Isles.

The Sassanids

By 200 AD the Parthians were facing a serious challenge from within their empire from the Sassanids, who take their name from Sasan, a predecessor of their leader Ardashir. Ardashir, though coming from a line of Mazdian priests, was of humble origins. But he was a shrewd leader, challenged Parthian rule and eventually conquered the whole of the Parthian Empire. Even before he ascended the throne in 226 AD he had himself crowned King of Kings, *Shahanshah,* and he built himself a luxurious palace at Firouzabad, near Fars.

Ardashir also saw himself as a direct descendant of the great Cyrus and King of Kings of a distinctly Persian, or Iranian Empire. As ruler of a new dynasty his aim was to eradicate the remaining Greek influence of the Seleucids and reinstate all things Persian. He first of all replaced the use of the Greek language with Persian. Of equal, if not more significance, he actively promoted the Persian religion of Zoroastrianism over against other religions. While he officially still permitted religious freedom, Zoroastrianism was clearly promoted as the official religion of the empire with other religions treated as subordinate.

The status of Zoroastrianism at this time, particularly in relation to kingship, is symbolised in the great rock carving at *Naqsh-e Rostom* near Persepolis. The carving, which can still be seen today, shows Ardashir seated on a horse receiving the symbol of divine kingship, in the form of a large ring, from the god *Ahura Mazda* who is also seated on a horse. Artabanus IV, the defeated Parthian king, is shown crushed beneath the hooves of Ardashir's horse and *Ahriman*, the God of evil is crushed beneath the hooves of *Ahura Mazda*'s horse. The message behind this symbolism suggests first, that good will always conquer evil and second, it signifies the divine status of the Sassanid king in the form of the symbolic ring of kingship, which is received from the god *Ahura Mazda*. In other words the act of passing the ring of kingship from *Ahura Mazda* confers divine status on the recipient, a concept that was to continue throughout Persian history.

Ardashir was succeeded by his son Shapur I, who ruled from 242 AD to 272 AD and was known as the Great. Although after 117 AD the Romans made no further attempts to extend their territory further into Persia, there were continuing clashes over border territory, especially in the region of Mesopotamia, Syria and Armenia. Shapur is best remembered for the humiliation he caused the Romans when he captured the Emperor Valerian at Edessa around 257 AD. Another famous rock carving at *Naqsh-e Rostom* celebrates this scene with Shapur I on horseback and Valerian kneeling in submission. It has also been suggested that Shapur used Valerian as a footstool as he mounted his horse, a task that Valerian performed for the rest of his life. While the reliability of this account could be questioned, there have been many artistic impressions of the event, for example, a watercolour by Hans Holbein in the 16th Century, which is currently in the *Kunstmuseum,* Basle.

Other accounts, and even rock carvings, show that Shapur I was magnanimous towards his captives. Certainly, he was tolerant when it came to religion and he had a particularly good relationship with the Jews. He was also supportive of Mani, the founder of Manichaeism, which was a syncretistic religion that contained elements of Zoroastrianism, Christianity and Buddhism. Manichaeism spread widely under the patronage of Shapur I but later

Kings took a less tolerant view and eventually it was declared heretical and Mani died in prison around 277 AD.

Another great Sassanid King was Shapur II who reigned from 309 AD to 379 AD. According to tradition he was crowned in his mother's womb, the crown being placed on his pregnant mother's stomach so ensuring his succession, while all other contenders for the throne were either blinded or murdered. This practice of getting rid of male contenders who were considered to be a threat to the throne, and therefore a threat to political stability, existed in the Persian, Byzantine and Ottoman empires for many centuries.

Shapur II was far less tolerant towards other religions than his predecessors and under his rule Zoroastrianism became the official religion of the empire. He commissioned the compilation of the *Avesta*, drawing together many of the ancient Zoroastrian texts and hymns into an official canon. Under his rule the persecution of Jews and particularly Christians became more prevalent. Shapur II's treatment of Christians possibly reflects what was happening at the time in the Eastern Roman Empire. Under the Roman Emperor Constantine, in around 324 AD Christianity became the official religion, and many Zoroastrians living in the Eastern Roman Empire found themselves as a persecuted minority. The Christianisation of Eastern Roman Empire also resulted in mass conversions across the Eastern Mediterranean including many soldiers of the Persian Empire, a situation that would be considered untenable by Shapur II.

As in previous centuries, conflict with the Romans Empire continued with large parts of the Eastern Mediterranean and Asia Minor passing backwards and forwards between the Roman Byzantines and Persians. However, at the death of Shapur II, in 379 AD, the Sassanid Empire was probably at its greatest extent, having conquered large parts of Byzantine territory.

The Sassanids were also renowned for their great achievements in art and culture, particularly under Khosrow II, who reigned between 590 AD and 628 AD. This was a period when many books were brought from India, chess was introduced, gardens were planted around beautiful palaces and one of the first Persian carpets, known as 'Spring of Khosrow' was commissioned for the palace at Ctesiphon. It measured 450 feet long and 90 feet wide and was woven in silk, gold and silver thread and embossed with rare stones. Unfortunately it was looted and cut up by Arab soldiers at the time of the Islamic conquest.

The Islamic Conquest

We have now come to a crucial period in the history of Iran, or Persia with the Islamic Conquest in the 7th Century. Prior to the conquest the Sassanid Empire and its vassal states stretched from the Indus Valley in the East, across Central Asia and around the Persian Gulf including the coastal area of the Arabian Peninsula. The Byzantines ruled the area of Anatolia and the Balkans.

When the Prophet Muhammad died in 632 AD, virtually the whole of the Arabian Peninsula was united under the banner of Islam and it was quite common at this time for Arab raiding parties to cross over into Persian territory. An Arab general named *Walid* successfully led one such party. He reported back to *Abu Bakr*, Muhammad's successor, who was the first Caliph of the *Rashidun* (Rightly Guided Ones), saying just how easy it was to cross into Persian territory, capture loot and then escape back into the Arabian desert. Consequently, *Abu Bakr* gave official permission for further raids to take place.

Walid then returned to Persia with 18,000 Arab warriors and within a short space of time he had conquered most of Mesopotamia, modern Iraq. In response, the Persian King *Yazdegerd III*, the last of the Sassanid Kings, called upon the Byzantines for help but even the combined forces of the Persians and the Byzantines could not keep the Arabs at bay. In 636 AD at the battle of *Qadisiyyah* the Persians were finally defeated. Ctesiphon was looted and most of the treasures taken back to Arabia. *Yazdegerd* fled to Merv in the North East of Iran and eventually died on the roadside after being robbed of all his possessions. One reason the Muslims were so successful at the time is because both the Persian Sassanids and the Byzantines were weak due to decades of fighting against each other. The Arabs, on the other hand, were fresh from the deserts and they also fought with a religious zeal believing that were doing the will of God.

The Zagros Mountains, which are a natural barrier between Iraq and Iran, became the boundary between the Muslim Arabs and the

Zoroastrian Persians. It is interesting to note that still today Iraqis, the inhabitants of what was Mesopotamia, see themselves as Arabs while the Iranians, although eventually conquered by Islam, maintained much of their Persian culture and particularly their Persian language.

The third *Rashidun* Caliph to succeed the Prophet Muhammad was *Uthman*, who reigned for 12 years during which time the Islamic conquest reached as far as Afghanistan in the East and around most of the North African coast. *Uthman* was assassinated in 656 AD and *Ali*, who was the Prophet's son-in-law and also his cousin, succeeded as fourth Caliph.

The Sunni/Shi'a Schism

We now come to another significant moment in the history of Iran, indeed in the history of worldwide Islam. When *Ali* died in 661 AD, also from assassination, there was disagreement within the Muslim community as to who should succeed. Some said that *Hasan*, the eldest son of *Ali,* had the right because he was a direct descendent of the Prophet Muhammad. Others claimed that *Muawiyah*, a member of the *Umayyad* tribe and also commander of the largest force at the time, was the rightful leader on the grounds that he was more experienced and commanded a larger following.

The conflict between the two came to a head when *Hussein, Ali's* second son was slaughtered along with most of the male members of his family. The date was 13th October 680 AD and the place was Karbala in modern Iraq. *Muawiyah* then became the first Caliph of the *Umayyad* Empire with its capital at Damascus.

From that time the supporters of *Ali* have been known as the *Shi'a*, 'the party of Ali', while those supporting *Muawiyah* became known as the *Sunni*, meaning 'People of the Tradition of the Prophet Muhammad and the consensus of the Islamic Community'.

The Battle of Karbala marked the first major schism within the Muslim world and many of the key locations of the conflict, for example Najaf, the burial place of *Ali* and particularly Karbala, the site of the massacre, have become places of pilgrimage for *Shi'a* Muslims across the world. Of interest to us is that for most of history these places were located within Greater Iran while now these locations are in Iraq. Consequently, people of Iran, now the largest *Shi'a* country in the world, have to travel to Iraq in order to visit their holy places.

Historically the *Sunnis* have made up about 90% of the worldwide Islamic community with the *Shi'a* representing approximately 10%. Of course, within both groups there is considerable diversity.

Chapter 3 Muslim Monarchies

The Abbasids

By the end of the 6th Century, on the eve of the Arab conquest, both the Sassanid Persians and the Byzantines were weakened by constant warfare. They were in a situation of stalemate and neither side were prepared for the surprise incursion of the Arabs. By 651 the Arabs had conquered the whole of Persia. However, conversion to Islam was slow, partly because it was discouraged on the grounds that non-Muslims had to pay a heavy tax, known as the *Jizya* tax. Mass conversion of the Persians would therefore have resulted in a loss of valuable revenue for the Arabs. On payment of this tax Christians, Jews and even Zoroastrians, all 'people of the Book' in Islamic eyes, were guaranteed protection and freedom of worship.

It should be stressed that while Persia had become a Muslim country by the end of the 7th Century, it was never Arabised. In other words, although it became Islamised in terms of religion, culturally Persia remained Persian. Unlike many other countries that came under Islamic rule, Persia never adopted Arabic as its common language. Persian and other Turkic languages remained in use albeit with the introduction of many Arabic words, particularly when it came to religion. The Arabs who first conquered Persia established garrison towns, rather as the Romans had done in earlier centuries. There was little integration between Persian and Arab and Persians were treated as second-class citizens. Eventually they came to resent their Arab overlords and it was only a matter of time before there was open rebellion.

This came in 750 when the descendants of Muhammad's youngest uncle, *Abbas*, who were *Shi'a*, rebelled. Known as the *Abbasids*, after Abbas, they overthrew the *Umayyads* and established a new Caliphate moving the capital from Damascus to Baghdad. Although initially the *Abbasids* were *Shi'a*, the Caliphate later chose to follow the *Sunni* tradition believing that this would make them more acceptable to the growing international Muslim community who were predominantly *Sunni*.

The *Abbasids* ruled from their capital in Baghdad from 750 until 1258, when the Mongols swept across Central Asia from the East destroying any city in their path that refused to surrender. Baghdad fell to the Mongols; her citizens were massacred and the Caliphate was transferred to Cairo.

The Islamic Golden Age

The *Abbasid* period is looked upon as a 'Golden Age' in terms of science and culture. At the same time, it was increasingly recognised throughout the known world as a power to be reckoned with. The *Abbasid Caliph al-Rashid*, for example, established good relations in the 8th Century with Charlemagne, also known as Charles the Great, ruler of the Carolingian Dynasty and regular diplomatic missions were exchanged between the two powers.

The *Abbasids* ruled over territory that had previously been part of the Greek Seleucid Empire and the successive Parthian and Sassanian dynasties preserved much of the Greek culture and scholarship of the Seleucids. When the Arabs arrived in Persia in the 7th Century they therefore inherited what the Persians had preserved: Greek philosophy, astronomy, mathematics, medicine, science and literature.

This wealth of learning was eventually translated from Greek into Arabic. So began a creative coming together of Arab, Persian, Greek and Indian culture that was eventually to be carried to Western Europe via Islamic Spain. From this point scholars were able to translate texts from Arabic into Latin so making ancient and valuable texts accessible to Western scholars, a process that in time contributed to the Renaissance. Similarly, Biblical and Patristic texts in the Greek language found their way via Constantinople from Byzantium to the West. Consequently, Western Biblical scholars had access to valuable texts in the original Greek language, a fact that influenced the unfolding of the Protestant Reformation in the 15th and 16th Centuries.

The first *Abbasid* Caliph, *Al -Rashid,* founded the 'House of Wisdom' in Baghdad and under his son *al Ma'mun*, who reigned from 813 to 833, this institution became the most famous in the Islamic world. Not only did it consist of a large library engaging in an ambitious translation programme, but it was also a research centre attracting scholars from across the known world. One such scholar was the Persian *ibn Sina*, known in the West as Avicenna. His most famous works are the *Book of Healing* and the *Canon of Medicine*, both of which were used in European universities as late as the 17th Century.

Astronomy had always been a specialism of the Persians. Traditionally, the 'Three Kings' or 'Wise Men from the Orient' who are mentioned in the Biblical nativity story are thought to have been astronomers from Persia. In the *Abbasid* period astronomy reached new heights.

Another great name of the period is *Omar Khayyam*, who was born in Nishapur, Khorasan in 1048. He is perhaps best known in the West as a poet and particularly as the author of the collection of poems known as the *Rubaiyat of Omar Khayyam*. Khayyam also made a significant contribution to the field of mathematics and especially algebra. He died in 1131 at the age of 82 and in 1963 the architect *Hooshang Seyhoun* designed a new mausoleum in his memory. Located in Nishapur, the town of the poet's birth, it is regarded today as a masterpiece of modern Iranian architecture.

Another important contribution to the Islamic Golden Age was in the field of literature and especially poetry. Among the great names we should mention is *Ferdowsi*, who lived from 940 to 1020. His greatest piece of work was the *Shahmaneh*, literally meaning the story of the Kings. It chronicles the stories of the pre-Islamic monarchies, celebrating the great deeds of Cyrus and Darius. Taking thirty years to complete, the *Shahmaneh* is today viewed as a masterpiece of world literature as well as a celebration of ancient Iranian or Persian identity before the Islamic conquest. Two other famous Persian poets were *Hafez* and *Rumi*. *Hafez*, who was born in Shiraz, lived from 1326 to 1390, which was just after the fall of the *Abbasids* to the Mongols. He is still a popular poet whose works can be found across the Turkish and Persian speaking countries today.

Jalal al-din Muhammad Rumi, known in the West as *Rumi*, stands in a class of his own. He was born in Tajikstan in 1207, at the end of the *Abbasid* period. *Rumi* was a poet, jurist and theologian and he was a *Sufi* mystic. The word *Sufi* comes from the word wool and early *Sufis* were known to wear woolen robes. *Sufism* is a mystical form of Islam that was popular at the time across Anatolia (modern

Turkey) and Persia. Its followers formed 'brotherhoods' from both *Sunni* and *Shi'a* traditions. *Rumi* believed that music, poetry and dance could all bring the devotee closer to God without the need for mosques and mullahs. These ideas led to the creation of the 'Whirling Dervishes' a group of dancers who slowly 'whirl' around each other in a trance-like state, the aim being to seek communion with God. Today *Sufis*, of all nationalities, can be found across the world and *Rumi's* poetry is still popular worldwide.

The *Abbasid* period spanned a period of almost five hundred years during which time Persia, or greater Iran became Islamicised but not Arabised. It was a time when the best of Arab, Persian, Turkish and even Indian culture came together culminating in what has been called the Islamic Golden Age. It was a time when medicine, philosophy, astronomy and mathematics reached new horizons. Eventually this knowledge reached Europe, either via the Muslim world of Spain or via Constantinople.

The Mongols

This high point of Islamic culture was disrupted by the invasion of the Mongols in 1258. Through military genius and brutal force, *Genghis Khan* united the many nomadic tribes of Mongolia and Eastern Asia, founding the Mongol Empire in 1206. He then began an aggressive campaign westwards across Asia. By 1368 the Mongols had reached the Mediterranean and much of Europe, destroying many cities along the way. In the process some Mongols settled and became assimilated with the local cultures. Others, however, returned to Mongolia.

By 1307 *Timur*, a descendent of *Ghengis Khan*, had taken most of North East Iran from the *Abbasids*. *Timur* was also known as *Tamerlane*, a corruption of *Timur* the Lame on account of his limp. He eventually came to rule a vast area across central Asia to the Persian Gulf, so establishing the *Timurid* Dynasty, which was to last until 1507. *Timur* was a great but ruthless leader. His multi-ethnic armies were feared across Europe, Asia and Africa for their brutality. It is said that his campaigns caused the death of some 17 million people. At the same time he enthusiastically embraced Islam and became a patron of the arts and sciences. A later descendent of

Timur, named *Babur*, was to cross from Afghanistan into Hindustan, where he founded the great *Mughal* Empire of India; *Mughal* being the Persian for Mongol.

By the beginning of the 16th Century the *Timurid* dynasty, as is the pattern in history, was beginning to disintegrate into small warring tribes. Into this political instability came a new power, the *Safavids*.

The Safavids

The *Safavid* dynasty, which ruled for almost two hundred years, from 1501 to 1736, marked an important turning point in both Islamic history and the history of Iran. *Shah Ismail I*, the founder of the dynasty, was only 14 years old when he came to the throne. He was born in Ardabil, North West Iran near the Caspian Sea. *Ismail*'s father was the sheikh of the *Sufi Safaviyya* Order, members of which were not only *Sufis*, but were also well trained and disciplined soldiers known as the *Qizilbash*. The *Qizilbash*, being a religious military order, could perhaps be compared to the medieval Knights Templar or Knights of St John. At one time *Ishmail* was the Grand Master of the *Qizilbash*.

As a devout *Shi'a Ismail* declared that *Shi'sm* should be the state religion of the country, an act that was to have a profound effect on the future of Iran. During his reign, he gave land and increasing powers to the clerics, established seminaries and imported *Shi'a* scholars from around the Levant.

The next *Safavid* Shah of significance was *Abbas*, known as the Great, who ruled from 1587 to 1629. His father had been a weak ruler who had lost territory in the East to Khorasan and the West to the Ottomans. *Abbas's* aim was to secure the empire and one of his first acts was to reduce the power of the *Qizilbash* who had far too much influence not just in the army, but also by virtue of holding top government positions.

In the place of the *Qizilbash Abbas* promoted another group, the *ghulams*, which means slaves. The *ghulams* were Georgian, Armenian and Circassian converts to Islam and they were given positions in the army and government administration, rather like the

Janissaries under the Ottomans. As with the *Janissaries*, the *ghulams* were loyal, able and well-disciplined soldiers.

When it came to military reform *Abbas* looked to Western Europe for assistance and he appointed two English brothers, Anthony and Robert Shirley, as military advisers. The act of appointing advisers from England is symbolic of how Iran saw herself at that time in terms of international relations.

The *Safavid* Empire, along with the Ottomans and the Mughals were three extremely powerful Muslim empires of the period, sometimes referred to as the Gunpowder Empires. The relationship between them was fickle. The *Safavid*s were *Shi'a*, located between two *Sunni* empires; the Ottomans and the Mughals. There were times when the Ottomans and the Mughals, both being *Sunni*, joined forces against the *Safavids*. There were also periods when the Mughals and *Safavids* enjoyed close relations, for example when the *Safavid Shah Tahmasp* gave refuge to the second Mughal Emperor *Humayan* in the 16th Century.

Another concern for the *Safavids* were the Afghan tribes, who were *Sunni*, and tended to swap allegiance between the India and Iran. Finally, there was the growing power of Russia in the North, who harboured ambitions of securing the warm sea ports of the Black Sea and, more worryingly for Iran, the southern coast of the Caspian Sea.

This was also a period when Persia became strategically important for other European powers. Once the Portuguese discovered a sea route around the coast of Africa and on to the East Indies, they needed safe ports where they could resupply their ships. The Persian Gulf was a perfect choice and the Portuguese were the first European power to establish bases in its protected waters. After initially receiving generous trade concessions from both Persia and Oman, the Portuguese came to dominate the sea-lanes to the detriment of the local inhabitants.

At the same time both the Dutch and the British were opening up their markets in Asia and particularly India and both countries were also keen to acquire safe ports of call *en route* from Europe to their trading colonies. The English traded through the English East India Company, which was founded in London in 1600 and by 1612

England had acquired trade concessions in India. By 1622 the Persians had tired of the Portuguese presence and appealed to the English for help in ousting them from the Gulf. In response four ships from the East India Company managed to clear the Straits of Hormuz of the Portuguese.

From another perspective, it was in the interests of the Western European countries to establish good relations with the Persians. This is because Western Europe's greatest threat at the time was the Ottoman Empire. The memories of the fall of Constantinople to the Ottomans in 1453 and the siege of Vienna by *Suleyman the Magnificent* in 1529 were still raw. The danger of Western Christendom falling to Islam was very real in the eyes of many Europeans. While *Safavid* Persia, being *Shi'a*, was not a natural ally of the Ottomans, it could provide an extremely useful ally to Europe, particularly considering its geographically strategic location.

These are just a few examples of how, by the 17th Century, Persia had become a player on the world scene. One consequence of this was that Europeans were now travelling to Persia and returning with tales of magnificent palaces complete with harems, opulent court life and markets filled with spices, silks and exquisite carpets. Another consequence was that Europeans were entering into trade agreements with the Persians, which, in the long run, were detrimental to the Persian economy. This was a pattern to be repeated over the following few centuries.

Shah Abbas was to be the last of the great *Safavid* rulers; those who followed him were weak and often despotic. Without a strong leader the economy declined and the country was vulnerable to attack on its borders; the Ottomans took parts of Mesopotamia, the Russians the Caucasus and the Afghans began chipping away at *Safavid* territory in the East.

By 1722 the Afghans managed to reach Isfahan, forcing the Shah to abdicate. There then followed a period of chaos until *Nadir Shah*, a former slave who had risen in the military ranks, managed reunite the country. *Nadir Shah* has been described as the Napoleon of Persia or a Persian Alexander the Great on account of his brilliant military achievements. In a short reign, from 1736 to 1747, he invaded the Mughal Empire and ransacked Delhi taking away a huge amount of booty including the famous *Koor e Noor* diamond, which is now part of the English crown jewels. He also reinstated territories that had previously been seized by the Ottomans or Russians.

The Qajars

The next Muslim monarchy of significance is that of the *Qajars*, a dynasty that lasted from 1782 until 1925. The *Qajars* were a Turkic tribal people who originated in North West Iran. The first *Shah*, *Mohammad Khan Qajar*, seized the throne in 1785 and made Tehran the capital.

Mohammad saw himself as another *Genghis Khan, Timur* or *Nadir Shah*. To his credit he did unite the country once more, after a period of instability, but at considerable cost to the people. He is remembered in history as perhaps the most cruel of all the rulers of Iran. On one occasion, in order to punish a rebellious town, it is said that he had the eyes of 20,000 men cut out. It has been suggested that his cruelty was due to his childhood when, at the age of six, his father was murdered and he was castrated on the orders of his uncle who feared the boy as a rival. For 16 years he lived as a hostage of a rival tribe. *Muhammad Qajar* was assassinated in 1796.

It should be pointed out that when it came to the question of succession, both the Ottomans and the Persians, and even the earlier Byzantines, followed similar practices. It was not unusual for brothers, nephews or male cousins to be killed, blinded or imprisoned in the harem in order to ensure that there would be no challenge to the throne.

As we move closer to the modern period the history of Iran becomes increasingly complex. During the *Qajar* period, European influence began to affect the lives of all Iranians, largely as a result of trade concessions that were offered by the *Qajar* monarchs to Europeans, mainly British, in exchange for princely sums of money. For example, the British were given a monopoly for the importation of cheap textiles that undercut local industry. During the reign of *Nasser al Din Shah*, who reigned between 1848 and 1896, two other monopolies were offered the British; one in tobacco and another for the building of railways and roads. In both cases the beneficiary was the King. Not only did the money in payment for the concession not filter down to the people, but the local industry, particularly the tobacco industry, suffered as a consequence imported tobacco.

Another consequence of this foreign involvement was that the powerful clerical constituency became highly critical of the Shah's policies. The clerics believed that the presence of Europeans, and there were an increasing number of them, would be detrimental to the religious culture of the country. As a result, the Shah was forced to cancel some of these concessions but this still didn't stop widespread rioting in protest across the country.

Probably the concession of greatest significance was offered to an Englishman William Knox D'Arcy in 1901. The concession granted D'Arcy exclusive rights to prospect for oil in Persia. In 1908 D'Arcy and his team struck a large amount of oil and the following year, in 1909, the Anglo-Persian Oil Company was formed. In return the Shah received £20,000 in cash, another £20,000 in shares and 16 per cent of the annual net profits.

During this period both Russia and Britain were competing for influence in Persia, but for different reasons. In 1907 they agreed to a 'truce' by dividing up the country into what has been called 'spheres of influence'. Russia was interested in control of the North and particularly the Caspian Sea while Britain wanted control of the South, not only because of the oil but also because of its strategic importance in relation to British India. On the eve of the First World War Russia and Britain were highly involved in Persia and the people were becoming increasingly opposed to the Shah and his policies. While the court squandered money, many starved. Protest groups formed and the key players in these groups were the intellectuals and the clerics; the mullahs who gained mass appeal through their network of mosques.

Chapter 4 The Modern Period

World War I

When the First World War broke out Persia claimed neutrality. Despite this the country became an arena for war with Ottoman, Russian and British troops fighting a proxy war on her soil. As a result, the people of Persia suffered all the horrors of war and the country suffered economically. When the Russian Revolution broke out in 1917 the Russians withdrew from Persia leaving Britain as the major foreign power in the country.

During the First World War, oil had replaced coal as the power supply for British ships and Britain's main concern was to maintain the control and security of the South of the country with its oil fields. *Ahmad Shah*, the last *Qajar* monarch, was ineffectual and he made himself extremely unpopular with his people by selling off valuable Persian resources to the West. The effects of the war led to the downfall of the *Qajars*.

In February 1921 *Ahmad Shah*, the last of the dynasty, was ousted in a military coup and was forced into exile with his family. He died in Paris in 1930. An officer of the Persian Cossack Brigade led the coup. His name was *Reza Khan* and he eventually became head of the *Pahlavi* dynasty, the last of the monarchies before the Iranian Revolution of 1979.

The Pahlavi Dynasty

Reza Khan was of humble origins. At 16 he joined the Persian Cossack Brigade, rose through the ranks and excelled as a military officer. He was said to be tall and good-looking but not particularly sophisticated or well educated. He was above all a strong Military man. In February 1921, he led the Cossack Brigade into Tehran and seized the throne from the *Shah*. He then became the Minister of War and in December 1925 was crowned monarch of a new dynasty, which he named *Pahlavi* after the ancient Iranian tribe.

Reza Shah's sole aim was to modernise the country, starting with the army, along Western lines, and he was very much influenced by Kemal Ataturk who was at that time following a similar process of Westernisation in Turkey. Some of *Reza Shah*'s initial policies included:

1. The introduction of conscription, which increased the armed forces.

2. Road building programmes, increasing 5,000 km of roads in 1927 to 24,000 km in 1938

3. Rail building programmes, increasing 250 km of rail line in 1925 to 1,700 km in 1938.

4. The expansion of education, which increased from 55,000 students in 1922 to 457,000 in 1938. However, this increase didn't include the rural areas, which remained neglected.

5. Iran, the ancient historical name used by the Iranians themselves, became the official name for the country and replaced the name Persia, which had been used by foreigners.

6. Foreign concessions, which had proved to be so unpopular with the people, were drastically reduced.

Another, extremely controversial, ruling was the forced abolition of the headscarf for women and replacement by Western headgear for both male and female. Consequently, some elderly women who had worn headscarves all their lives, preferred to stay at home. Younger women who were uncomfortable not wearing a headscarf missed out on work and educational opportunities. Women at the higher end of the social strata however benefited greatly.

Reza Shah's main justification for seizing power was to rid the country of foreign influence that was so detrimental to the wellbeing of ordinary Iranians. He believed that the *Qajars* had sold the soul of Iran to foreigners for financial benefit; the sole beneficiary being the monarchy, which he claimed was despotic and corrupt, while the people starved. As a consequence, *Reza Shah* was vehemently anti British and anti-Russian but he still needed Western expertise if he was to bring Iran up to modern standards.

His neighbour, Turkey, with whom he was on good relations, had benefitted from German expertise and so he also looked to the Germans for help. During the latter half of the 1930s, hundreds of German engineers and technicians entered Iran. With the outbreak of the Second World War, and particularly after Germany had invaded Russia in 1941, the presence of Germans on the ground in Persia posed a threat both to Britain and Russia. Both countries therefore asked *Reza Shah* to expel the Germans. When he refused to do so an Anglo-Soviet force invaded the country and forced the abdication of the *Shah* in favour of his son *Mohammad Reza Shah*.

Most of us will remember *Mohammad Reza Pahlavi*, the last *Shah* of Iran, if for nothing else, but for his beautiful wives. His first wife, whom he married in 1939, was *Fawzia* of Egypt, who once appeared on the front cover of Life Magazine. But the marriage was not a success and they divorced in 1948. In 1951 the Shah married for a second time; to *Soraya*, daughter of an aristocratic family. The wedding was extremely lavish and the marriage said to be happy but once more, this time due to the inability of *Soraya* to produce a child, the couple divorced. The Shah's third wife was *Farah*. They were married in 1959, and had four children; three girls and one boy. *Reza Pahlavi*, the son, is the current Head of the House of Pahlavi. Queen *Farah*, widow of *Muhammad Reza Shah*, currently lives in the United States and Egypt. She is extremely active in charitable work and often attends international celebrity events such as the wedding of Prince Albert II of Monaco.

Muhammad Reza Shah was not at all like his father, who was from a poor background but through the military was able to rise to power. *Reza Shah* had been harsh, determined and ambitious. In contrast, *Muhammad* had benefited from an excellent education and had a sharp mind but he was shy and indecisive.

During *Muhammad's* first few years of rule, between the war years of 1941 to 1945, the country was still occupied by the Russians and the British. At the end of the War Britain, and later Russia, withdrew. By this time *Muhammad*, like his father, had become anti British and anti-Russian.

During the Second World War, America had entered the stage and it was to America that the young *Shah* looked for help, both financial and practical. So began what became a close relationship between the last *Shah* of Iran and the United States of America, whereby the *Shah* accepted huge loans from the United States for the construction of ambitious technical and building works. Many of these projects were of a military nature and included the technology capable of producing nuclear power. Consequently, hundreds of American technicians with their families entered the country. They were given diplomatic immunity and enjoyed all the benefits of diplomatic status.

From the beginning of the 20th Century there had been various attempts at constitutional reform in the country but there were constant setbacks, often because the monarchy was unable to accept dissent in any form. Political opposition groups, liberal intellectuals and frequently out-spoken clerics were brutally suppressed by the newly formed SAVAK, Iran's secret police. Even government ministers whose policies didn't suit the *Shah* mysteriously disappeared or were murdered. For example, when the democratically elected Prime Minister *Mohammad Moseddegh* proposed the nationalisation of Iran's oil in 1953, he was deposed, imprisoned and died under house arrest. It is generally believed that both the CIA and MI6 were involved, albeit at a distance, the reason being that the nationalisation of Iran's oil would not be in the interests of either the USA or Britain.

The Iranian Revolution

The majority of Iranians viewed the Pahlavi monarchy, along with many earlier monarchies, as being corrupt and despotic. However, another element now entered the equation; the United States of America. Many believed that *Muhammad Reza Shah* was simply a puppet of America, which was deeply resented, especially by the clergy who feared that Iran's culture and especially its Islamic values were under threat from foreign, and particularly American, Western influence.

It was into this context that one young cleric by the name of *Ruhollah Moosavi Khomeini* began making a name for himself. Later known as the *Grand Ayatollah Khomeini*, in 1979 he became the first Supreme Leader of the Islamic Republic of Iran. *Khomeini* was born in 1902 and began studying the Koran and ancient Persian at the age of six. He became an accomplished scholar and went on to teach at the Islamic seminary of *Qom*, the largest and probably the most prestigious seminary for *Shi'a* scholarship in the world. He taught political philosophy, Islamic history and ethics and he produced numerous writings on Islamic philosophy, law, and ethics. He was also interested in mysticism. His public persona was one of grim severity but according to those close to him there was another, warmer side to his personality which was especially evident when among family and close friends.

Khomeini's religious views were firmly based upon *Shi'a* Islam and the *Sharia* Law, with its strong emphasis on equality, justice and the rights of the poor. Justice and honesty had also been central to the earlier Zoroastrian religion and was therefore deeply embedded in traditional Iranian values. *Khomeini*'s political views were formed against the background of two world wars and what he considered foreign intervention. He believed that the Western influence and close relationship with the United States was a challenge to the sovereignty and the religious values of Iran. *Khomeini* was charismatic and articulate and he began preaching against both foreign influence and a weak and corrupt monarchy that squandered the resources of the country while the people starved.

At a time when political groups were firmly suppressed, the vast network of mosques became the vehicle through which *Khomeini*'s voice reached hundreds of thousands of people from all walks of life. In this way he drew support from the masses and his political views were spread across the country and particularly among the rural poor. Eventually he was arrested and imprisoned on several occasions. Finally, in 1964 he was sent into exile. During his period of exile, he continued to preach and teach and still had a great following in Iran. At the same time, many other groups were calling for political reform and the removal of the *Shah*. Rioting and protest movements were brutally put down; hundreds were imprisoned, tortured or executed.

By January 1979 the country was in turmoil and finally the *Shah* and his family were forced to leave Iran, ostensibly on holiday. However, they never did return. The Shah at the time was suffering from fairly advanced cancer and the family went to the United States for treatment. On the 1st February *Ayatollah Khomeini* returned to Tehran from France on a chartered Air France Boeing. He was welcomed at the airport by a rapturous crowd of hundreds of thousands.

The *Shah* underwent treatment for cancer when he arrived in the States but there were voices among the revolutionaries in Iran who called for his return in order to face criminal charges. The United States was accused of sheltering the *Shah* and Anti American feelings grew. On the 4th November 1979, a group of students occupied the American Embassy and held 54 American citizens for 444 days. The film, *Argo*, tells the story well.

The inability of the US President Jimmy Carter to resolve the hostage crisis contributed to his downfall and the consequent election of Republican Ronald Reagan. The hostages were released on the 20th January 1981, the very same day that Reagan was sworn into Office. It is generally believed that a deal had been made between Iran and the incoming administration whereby the hostages would be released in exchange for the provision of arms to Iran. This came to be known as the Iran-Contra Affair.

The Iran-Iraq War

The exile of the *Shah* in February 1979 and his death the following September marked the end of monarchical rule in Iran. The return of *Ayatollah Khomeini* marked the beginning of a *Shi'a* Islamic State ruled as a theocracy known as the Islamic Republic of Iran. From now on the country was to be ruled according to Islamic Law. As with all revolutions, there were reprisals with hundreds of ex government officials being executed and thousands, particularly political dissidents and intellectuals, leaving the country.

Khomeini preached of a resurgent *Shi'a* Islam, almost a renaissance that he believed would quickly spread across the region. This naturally caused concern to the surrounding countries, which were mainly *Sunni*. Iraq, already in dispute over its borders with Iran, had the most to fear. *Saddam Hussein*, President of Iraq, feared that there would be an uprising among the *Shi'a* population of his own country leading to a similar revolution in Iraq.

On the 22nd September 1980 Iraq invaded Iran, believing that the *Sunnis* of Iran would come over to the side of Iraq. This didn't happen; the Iranian *Sunnis* remained loyal to their country. Despite the fact that Iraq had better equipment, Iran, with its vast human resource, had virtually won the war by the following year. However, hostilities dragged on for a further six years, largely due to foreign involvement. During this time Iraq used chemical weapons resulting in the death of over 100,000 Iranians.

The United States and other European countries also feared the idea of *Shi'a* Islam spreading across the region, which could lead to destabilization. In 1984 United States President Reagan prohibited, by executive order, all trade with Iran. This was to be the beginning of many sanctions imposed on the country. By August 1988, when a ceasefire between Iran and Iraq was finally agreed, over 500,000 soldiers and civilians on both sides had lost their lives.

Ayatollah Khomeini died in 1989, just after the ceasefire, and was succeeded by *Hoseyni Khamenei* as Supreme Leader. *Khamenei* had previously held the post of President and had also fought in the Iran-Iraq war. As *Grand Ayatollah, Khamenei* has supreme power over all overseas and domestic policy. He is described as a conservative. For example, he declared that the study of music and the arts in universities is un-Islamic and that the wearing of the *hijab* should be made compulsory. At the same time, he supports stem cell research and is known to have intervened at times against the death sentence.

Probably the most controversial figure of the recent Iranian government was President *Mahmoud Ahmadinejad*. Coming from a poor background he trained as an engineer and teacher, becoming Mayor of Tehran in 2003. It has been suggested that he was among the students involved in the Hostage crisis of 1979 but the Establishment has always denied this. *Ahmadinejad* is known for his outspoken criticism of the West, particularly Israel, the UK and the USA. He was also a strong supporter of the Iranian nuclear programme. His election for a second term of office as President led to riots because a large proportion of the population had voted for his opponent who was a reformist candidate. When he won the election, there were accusations of ballot rigging. *Ahmadinejad* was unpopular and frequently accused of corruption. At one time, he was summoned by the Islamic Consultative Assembly to defend certain of his actions but for most of the time he still managed to maintain the support of *Khamenei*.

Under the Iranian Constitution the post of President is limited to just two terms of office and therefore at the end of his second term *Ahmadinejad* was forced to step aside. *Hassan Rouhani,* who is generally considered to be a moderate reformist succeeded to the post of President on the 13th June 2013.

A Nuclear Threat?

As early as 1947, soon after *Muhammad Reza Shah* came to the throne, the United States and Iran signed a 'Mutual Defense Assistance Agreement', which is still in force today. Between 1957 and 1975, the United States provided equipment and technical assistance for the Iranian nuclear programme. This included weapons grade uranium and plutonium. In 1968 Iran signed the Nuclear Non-Proliferation Treaty. In 1981, as part of the Iran-Contra deal, Iran received military hardware and nuclear technology from the United States.

All the above points show that there was a time when Iran and the US had good relations. Furthermore, the US supplied Iran with conventional armaments and also the equipment and technical knowhow in order for Iran to produce nuclear power. However, apart from the Iran-Contra deal in 1981, all this support was offered during the time of the *Shah*. In other words, ever since the Revolution of 1979, the US and its allies have been vehemently opposed to Iran possessing nuclear power. While Iran has permitted Inspectors into the country, and *Khamenei* has made repeated statements that Iran is not interested in acquiring such weapons which would be against Islamic law, there is still a suspicion in the West that Iran is following a secret programme aimed at building nuclear weapons. The fear of the West is that should Iran succeed in producing such weapons they may get into the hands of unstable governments and particularly groups such as the *Shi'a Hezbollah* based in Lebanon; a situation that would pose a serious threat to Israel.

Since 1979 the US has placed numerous trade sanctions on Iran including the freezing of Iranian assets. Pressure has also been placed on other countries that might consider trading with Iran. However, Russia and China have resisted this. Between 2010 and 2012 at least four Iranian nuclear scientists have been assassinated and Iran has suffered cyber attack; in all cases Iran suspects that the CIA may be involved. What seems to be quite clear from the above is that whilst the West, and especially the US, were quite happy for a *Pahlavi* monarchy, albeit unpopular and corrupt, to possess nuclear weapons, it cannot tolerate an Islamic state such as Iran having the same right.

Epilogue

On the 15th June 2013 *Hassan Rouhani* was democratically elected President of Iran, so replacing *Mahmoud Ahmadinejad*. *Rouhani*, who is considered to be a 'moderate' compared to his predecessor, is a cleric who studied at the prestigious seminary at Qom in Iran and later at Glasgow Caledonian University. He was previously Deputy Speaker of the Iranian Parliament and also led the Iranian team in negotiations with the UK, France and Germany on Iran's nuclear programme.

During the election campaign *Rouhani* declared that if elected his priorities would be to restore the economy and improve relations with the West. In many ways, these are two sides of the same coin because hopefully if he can open up a dialogue with the West that may result in the removal of sanctions, which in turn would benefit the economy.

Since his election his domestic policy has been reformist despite some resistance from the conservative clerical body. He has promoted greater personal freedom and improved access to information. He has also supported the rights of women and appointed women to ministerial posts.

When *Rouhani* took up his position as President on Saturday 3rd August 2013 the Syrian Civil War had already been raging for two years. The United States was on the brink of attacking Syria in response to alleged chemical attacks by President Assad's regime against his own people. Other Western powers, including Britain were showing far more caution, with the British Parliament eventually voting not to intervene militarily.

At the same Syria's ally Russia was calling for a diplomatic solution through dialogue. President *Rouhani* publicly endorsed Iran's position calling for dialogue alongside that of Russia. Iran was speaking out but having been ostracised by the West since 1979 her voice was hardly heard.

Since that time the situation in Syria has gone from bad to worse. Hundreds of thousands of innocent men women and children have fled the conflict creating a sea of refugees seeking asylum in

Since 1979 the US has placed numerous trade sanctions on Iran including the freezing of Iranian assets. Pressure has also been placed on other countries that might consider trading with Iran. However, Russia and China have resisted this. Between 2010 and 2012 at least four Iranian nuclear scientists have been assassinated and Iran has suffered cyber attack; in all cases Iran suspects that the CIA may be involved. What seems to be quite clear from the above is that whilst the West, and especially the US, were quite happy for a *Pahlavi* monarchy, albeit unpopular and corrupt, to possess nuclear weapons, it cannot tolerate an Islamic state such as Iran having the same right.

Epilogue

On the 15th June 2013 *Hassan Rouhani* was democratically elected President of Iran, so replacing *Mahmoud Ahmadinejad*. *Rouhani*, who is considered to be a 'moderate' compared to his predecessor, is a cleric who studied at the prestigious seminary at Qom in Iran and later at Glasgow Caledonian University. He was previously Deputy Speaker of the Iranian Parliament and also led the Iranian team in negotiations with the UK, France and Germany on Iran's nuclear programme.

During the election campaign *Rouhani* declared that if elected his priorities would be to restore the economy and improve relations with the West. In many ways, these are two sides of the same coin because hopefully if he can open up a dialogue with the West that may result in the removal of sanctions, which in turn would benefit the economy.

Since his election his domestic policy has been reformist despite some resistance from the conservative clerical body. He has promoted greater personal freedom and improved access to information. He has also supported the rights of women and appointed women to ministerial posts.

When *Rouhani* took up his position as President on Saturday 3rd August 2013 the Syrian Civil War had already been raging for two years. The United States was on the brink of attacking Syria in response to alleged chemical attacks by President Assad's regime against his own people. Other Western powers, including Britain were showing far more caution, with the British Parliament eventually voting not to intervene militarily.

At the same Syria's ally Russia was calling for a diplomatic solution through dialogue. President *Rouhani* publicly endorsed Iran's position calling for dialogue alongside that of Russia. Iran was speaking out but having been ostracised by the West since 1979 her voice was hardly heard.

Since that time the situation in Syria has gone from bad to worse. Hundreds of thousands of innocent men women and children have fled the conflict creating a sea of refugees seeking asylum in surrounding countries and beyond. Many have drowned in the Mediterranean Sea. Thousands have suffered untold hardship trekking through mud and snow across Europe only to find barbed wire and walls blocking their way.

Thousands more are still trapped in 'camps' in countries such as Greece, Turkey and France. And millions more in Syria are either displaced or held captive at the brutal hands of *Daesh*. At the time of writing (December 2016) the ancient city of Aleppo is about to be annihilated by the Government forces of Syria and her ally Russia.

Throughout the Syrian crisis Iran has supported President Assad and his Government forces. While the majority of Syrians are *Sunni*, President Assad together with many of his Government officials and supporters are *Alawite Shi'a*. Although Syria is not a theocracy as is Iran, the *Alawites* and Iranians share a common religious identity in *Shi'a* Islam. For the same reason the Lebanese *Hezbollah* are also supportive of the Syrian Regime.

Initially Iran offered President Assad advisory, technical and financial support. That has now been extended to include the training of Syrian combat troops and provision of Iranian troops to fight on Syrian soil. Both Russia and Iran claim to be supporting President Assad in his fight again *Daesh* and other Islamist groups. However, both Russia and Iran are also open about their desire to keep the current Syrian regime in power. This policy automatically puts Russia and Iran on a collision course with the West and Turkey who openly seek the collapse of the Assad regime.

While the Syrian crisis rumbled on there were efforts behind the scenes to improve relations between the United States and Iran. For example, both President Obama and President *Rouhani* were supportive of the Iran Deal that was approved on the 14th July 2015. Formally known as the *Joint Comprehensive Plan of Action,* the Deal was an international agreement between Iran and the P5+1 (five members of the United Nations Security Council - France, China, United Kingdom, United States and Russia - plus Germany) and the European Union.

Under the terms of the Agreement Iran agreed to restrict her nuclear programme for a period of 13 years. In exchange, and provided that she abided by the Agreement, Iran would have certain economic sanctions lifted. It would appear that President *Rouhani's* commitment at his election to both improve relations with the West and restore the Iranian economy were about to be fulfilled.

However, since the signing of the Iran Deal in July 2015, there have been major changes to the political scene across Europe and in the United States. With the election of Donald Trump as President Elect in the United States future relations with Iran are questionable and the Iran Deal with its long hoped for loosening of economic sanctions looks extremely fragile.

****

About the Author

Anne has had a life-long interest in history and the religions of the world. This led to her studying both topics for her first Degree and later for her Doctorate. She spent several years living overseas and this experience added to her fascination with different peoples and cultures.

For many years, she was Adviser in Inter Religious Relations with the Church of England. She was also Vice Moderator of the Dialogue Unit of the World Council of Churches in Geneva and has sat on numerous advisory bodies for Inter Religious Relations around the world.

Anne is an accredited lecturer with the National Association of Decorative and Fine Arts. She also lectures regularly on cruise ships and at academic institutions around the United Kingdom.

http://www.annedavison.org.uk